WHEN MONKEYS FEEL RHYTHMS

MICHAEL P AMRAM

Order this book online at www.trafford.com
or email orders@trafford.com

Most Trafford titles are also available at major online book retailers.

Printed in the United States of America.

ISBN: 978-1-4907-3772-0 (sc)
ISBN: 978-1-4907-3773-7 (e)

Trafford rev. 06/06/2014

 www.trafford.com

North America & international
toll-free: 1 888 232 4444 (USA & Canada)
fax: 812 355 4082

CONTENTS

III POLITICS

IV FRIENDSHIP

V MARRIAGE

VI AGEING

VII Technology

To my wife Deborah;
To causal relationships
Tangent or benign….

To evolution's breaths
That leaves air encrypted
To seed a poet's mind

I
SPATIAL RELATIONSHIPS

MEANDERING UP TO TIME

your cadenced swings
reminded me of a
pendulum hung to
swell the time
you spent pumping legs;
brilliant and measured—
a park swing cinched its way
around you;

pig-tails would follow you
and pass by quickly,
saluting greenery
of corkscrew
jungle-gym poles built
just to feel your glides,
dug deep in wood chips lain
thick to dare;

you to swing higher,
to jump and hug the sun;
or someone who could catch
baseball's thrown
past the greens keeper's
tractor tending his sod,
cleaning the mound for late
pitcher's nods;

you soared over the
tanned concession house where
hot dog vendors gathered once
for the game;
now your sling's hung low,
its chains are twisted so
that playground will know it's
summers end.

TIMING OPPORTUNITY RIGHT

I feel my left foot;
it is hideous and deformed,
with ridges all linear
like the Rocky Mountain's
Flat Irons can boast;

I press my foot's thick
yellowed nails in the spaces jammed
in doors with its cracked footprints
that bunions giants
left for me to trace;

I'll nurture my foot
with my opposable thumbs;
I'll massage it bloodless 'til
fists cramp and swell up like
dough that's out too long;

I'll elevate my foot—
prop it coolly on my desk and
recline in my leather chair
like an executive
so I'll kill two birds;

while some ice packs wait
to deflate my monstrous foot
and tempt its toes to wiggle,
to make me step lightly
and stick my toe

across threshold lines
with the large plastic boots made for
fractured walking that's found in
finite, ensemble casts
whose shadows giggle;

and wiggles begin
to pick at toes that I left jammed;
I'll stick my ashen scaly
foot in doors before they
warp too swell and close.

GLOBAL POSITIONING

the paper was corrugated
in the WC in Leeds,
England, UK, so I sat
futilely pondering 53°
47 north, 1° 32 west,
my position globally;

it was gray and coarse; so I
sat humming silently
in a water closet;
trains bore through as I sat
on a platform closer to me
in Leeds station house;

I heard trains invigorate as
they came, raging like angered
bees, swarming around boundaries
that anointed to crown me;
I listened for them to become
crescendos in their distance,

they achieved thunderous clattering
and the wheels screeched so loud;
muffled voices had earned
my appeal as they'd direct me
where the stations would have
soft paper in their WC.

MICHAEL P AMRAM

SANITY OF BUTTERFLIES

a piece-meal sun bore past
pin-holes boxing my light;
it leads windowed cells to
feet that could tread well on the
lucid cracks on beams that would
hang me, learning to fly
right in my strait- jacket world;

my palms crossed like leaves blown
insane with autumn rain;
my fingers then would fold
swollen white with fear, wrinkled
and knuckled weak from swallowed
pride and despair checked at
your steel doors six weeks ago;

"I couldn't breathe……"
shit, "I couldn't yell….."
but no one cared that I
gathered no air from my cells;
my heart beat like a drum and
the jacket soaked straighter
with sweat that's sipped by demons;

they raised their glasses to
me, the scant men in white
coats waving nets that flowed
down the straight and narrow paths
I had groomed to let them see;

the hairs they'd find matted
with my flop sweat to gel it;

my demons netted me,
adding to their collected
works of insects that fly
free with wings curved right from well
spent wear in a case under
glass I might choose to break
should I remember despair.

POCKETING LANGUAGE

I buried deep my knee-length socks
intensely to soften pain;
I wheeled my chair closer so
the sharp cold could constrict my veins;
I knelt with my pack icing
the swells that could hear me call;
coaxing slight lilts out of gaits
they'd hold for me if I fell;
silent like a loon that would cross
placid waters without flight
savings of sounds that echo space
and pray for things time has lost;

I'd get ahead of sounds I knew,
my feet numbing down for them;
gluttons for maliciousness
my mind condemns for hoping;
riding rules no one will hear
in long-leggings worn for battle
they confront eyes, fixed judging ice
as piercing stares find the seals
of pedestrian clothes I'd tear
like Velcro straps that might slip
if ripping sounds grew to loud
when stuffing hosiery.

WHEN EASELS FIT THE GALAXY

a potter felt callouses thrown
like those he'd kiln;
for colors that had sight
and bowls of earthy red cracked too
soon, like blisters
they oozed; and puss would form
the lava fields at night;

when stratospheres were crossed to fuse
the brightest stars;
eclipse the moon in shafts
of the light years that were saved,
then artists' hands
felt faces until they
could push his fingers back;

and he saw knuckles white as sheets
to hide the motes
that bridged reality;
with a universe shaped to fuse
in the kilns that
leave trace amounts of ash
on which Milky Way's muse;

it ponders canyons' erosion
futilely, it
defends stars that must be;
it would wander eternally
for some names of

prodigal sons that wrote
or drew crude things to see;

sent back to times when wars were fought
just to win rights
to brag, so men could dream
how cold mars might be
as they scribbled their notes;

when sons were wiser than the
father claimed he'd
be; so poet's pens set
free the stars, easels grew to fit
their galaxies;
roads could use toes to count
dead, squishing, muddied souls;

they're left behind to bleed earth red;
coagulate
and shed peelings for earth's
crust, erasing time artists wait
for clays to form
and holds them hostage like
a message floats at sea;

marbles spin to blue to conjure
tranquility;
oceans reserved to ease
gifted hands teaching misery
to swim between
moated pools spiraling
down—breaking all the rules.

TRYING TO SHRINK THE UNIVERSE

he sought treasure in an onion,
elusive riddles lining its core;
deep between skins of sadness
that steal tears from your eyes that wore
ways of tomorrow's fortunes;
the fickle picks dreams should show
to blind dancing eyes caught peeking
inside peels of seeds to know
onion skins time will assuage;

raptures rid the morality,
and sooth uncertainty you feel;
it's a tapped pail, hollow steel
wrapped in the centers of great minds;
happy stories chose the middle
ground to learn to fit your head;
for tear drains onions grieve,

ducts high on paths from which we're led
with knives in hand to reveal;

slipping silent, knives know their fame
won by coring what nature knew;
a talisman for trying,
for abetting altruistic hands;
bleeding answers they once grew
with parchment white as onions
of purple as breaths left pain

the thinner skins that paled on
the onion rings that remained;

the fortune's told like an onion
from cookies Chinese places give;
with take-out food that made it
to the believers that would hide
fruited plants of promise that
find where eccentric slayers live;
and peel deeper past the anguish
the fiercest rage you once knew,
saving hurts to never yell;

feigned as bells begin to chime;
and sound beyond the onion fields,
tapped with wires too thin to string
eyes that cry to mince— their words
confess what was lost before;

and fortunes find less repentant ones
that kneel alone in onion fields;
for answers to conundrums
that pry and tear at eyes to cry;
peeling layers to thin their skin
like times contrived to lose the wins
and fences that would hold their pain;
for dying onions in the sun.

SIMCHA QUEENED IOWA

she's Union, the
good railroad engineer;
a slave steam boat pilots
could hush one day;

when fugitives
would run along banks that
missed the boats just in time
to free the wheel's

sounds that splash 'round
to twain, and Huck and Jim
would raft for Cairo's lights
to find their fame;

Sim queened the Miss.—
mightier than the boats
and gospel ghosts on banks
of Iowa;

she bides time's sigh,
crossing to lead mines of
Galena where Ulysses'
horse used to ride;

the river's owed
narrows for fantastic
trips guided by three stars
hung noosed to dip;

MICHAEL P AMRAM

Sim's a blessing,
an heiress to barges' holds;
she hears water rushing so
her story's told.

THE EPIC MENAGERIES

clouds formed pleasingly,
with darkness eclipsing
heaven's holes to mock the sun;
the sky kept feeling like

the world's going to change—
for better or worse;

shadows they cast are fitted,
encrypted for clouds too
soggy to hold rain;
bridles clatter with hoofs
that beat just sixteen counts;
as you listen hard,

they're seen last leaving drops
of rein bits in murky skies;
while you pray for the
apocalypse and forget
the world promised to change;

for better or worse—

so still you prayed
and soon you knelt,
rain came harder so
God just played cards that
we all were dealt;

you went at it again
and kept missing His saves—

you'd mock stronger winds
and trees that would fall
as you tried to be brave;

clouds were less pleasing, they'd
sift existentially
past eyes held open
wide for pies and horse's hoofs
that prick the sky so you'll
wonder what life's worth.

INTERNAL INVESTMENTS

I was young and they claimed
roller coasters were safe;
I could buy some fun if I
would ride their shining rails;

my teeth slit for Chiclets' chew
and their swallows' rise, and
then my stomach swelled to know
the bile burning me;

but my hand was held to start,
to lead me to him;
a carne who closed the deal
his tattooed arms, paled and slimmed,
a greasy smile worn;
it assured me every
ticket sold was worth its
wait with no refunded ones;

a bar then tousled
me while the carne grinned with his
two missing front teeth and
my ascent began—so
I thought of twists ahead;
I calculated three
moments I'd bought to dread;

the coaster
ticked- tacked to

chagrin of tracks with
steal that squeaked as we
rolled faster to reprieve their bend:

then it pulled…
and *clattering* paused
a bit for me, a break
for my lip—it clicked relentless
to the
top;

my eyes opened—
the park spreads out
for moments to view;

the car tilts down, it lifts weightless
again my stomach flips me;
now illusorily it
sends the coaster to
dove-tail spins that play with
centrifugal
force…

it was over, a carne grins
like it'd been a bad dream;
and I felt the earth for
its mercy's gravity.

A CENTRIFUGE FOR THE BUG-BOY

for every construction, destruction is built
every procrastination bears retention
every reluctance learns acceptance
every resistance begs acquiescence;

a world dies, a day evens
the score; randomly recoups
no less or more;

no more…

every hypocrisy finds truth somewhere
every pontification nurtures resistance
every civil disobedience tries patience
every promise broken kneads karma;

so what's gained when we lose?
like placing random boys on
mounts would tender shoes;

for every assassination, there's defamation
every assimilation needs concession
every proclamation fuels oppression
every conflagration owes a peace;

even as it's become,
global bugs that can comfort one;
who'll click his heels?

to run—

every legislation spawns incarnation
every invention gets a reincarnation
every conception has an abortion
every prohibition loses;

every determination has its day
every consternation ends in epiphany
every motive hides its ulterior
every discovery finds opposition;

so bug- boys grasp frothy
manes, high in stirrups they ride
prodding bellies;

every desolation offers direction
every recalcitrance owes its shame
every reticence wins gregarious
grins to tame;

when fobbing reins, bugs
watch to wake man with their crops
that dig for ends;

too slow, too fast;
for every death comes birth,
the race is never won.

A MID-WEST MANIFESTO

I'd like to burn the streets
and consume them in flames;
I want sleep to melt in
pillowed sheets as my dreams
burn the drifts silently;

I'd kill the vengeful flakes

trapped in the snowy globes;
my eyes now wander to
the winded chimes that ring
hollow, nameless streets like
the clocks that tick sometimes;

I stare long, down empty
streets with icy glares and
know nature's joke on me;
so I'll skate across the
rinks and shatter what was
conceived to be;

I want napalm in
November to last
until the spring, to rid
the land of nature's hand
that's learned to count past three;

like Vietnam in pieces
of light that falls through trees

with shades of spiders feeling
up the paths that led to leaves;

I'll wish bagging clouds combust
and explode the sun with burns;
thundering from hands gloved
with fingers numb to pain,

flames those throwers knew
fired fast down lanes that
cringed when they saw
their name.

TOE PRINTS IN AUGUST
(1977)

carvings stretched like pennies
imbedded in their walks,
wooded with oaken scents;
as I read ancient names,
I'd swivel my head back
around to look again:

we left Mantorville when
these planks splintered the night,
and sun repressed our time;
mom and I passed Mayo—
ten minutes out of town
the radio fell silent;

a man delivered news,
he told us Elvis died;
then silence followed us
eighty miles; the wheat fields
waved singing "I'm all shook up"

and I cried to mute them;
I felt my toe again
to ease me from my pain;
my foot toed the dash,
I was no Elvis fan—
of his famous lines to see
all Memphis's graceful lands;

"my mama always told me…"
he said in a song once
knowing as mothers can be;
his name was trod to stain heels
in Mantorville's street lights glean;
then they'd bow dolefully,
the "king" was dead and my
toe would always know when
pain etched my memory.

SQUEEZE PLAY

as a parting gift
I received an accordion
file, they gave me
it in lieu of severance pay;
I'd collate my
job regrets to recite
its alphabet;
printed in black stenciled letters
on its numbed dog-eared
corners; it was thin and blue from
cardboard parasites
staring at me to learn and play
the "lady of Spain"
medley; I could adopt a
monkey and teach it
to dance and earn nickels for me,

we'd busk in tube halls;
in Bishops Gate wind from trains'
tubing ruffled us
to smile wry with teeth in cheek:

that blue file sat,
surmising me and my monkey
traits I knew somehow,
in vacant corners of my room;

it would face the wall
like naughty apes that get time outs

to consider what's real,
Spanish women and monkey's that
slip banana peels
as they dance to their collated steps
to masticate that
banana's chew just right—I'd think

of scenarios
accordant to terminal jobs;
I finally tossed it
in a dumpster because
it didn't play well;
I wanted my monkey back,
those bananas and
the change that found ways to my hat.

IN ANY EVENT

she commented
"I'm not going to live forever,"
and then tagged her bags
for travel;

her life receded
to swipe a smile from her
lips that warned the
baby-boomers

of the complacency;
when life was still
an honest game
of flattering leaves to move

baggage that knew it came
like lava lamps, the
bags wait chilly at her door
with crumpled tags

she saved for some afterlife,
and worms could fill her mouth
like Himmler tongued the
cyanide tabs to rest,

to rob the Shabbos Goyish
flame lighters of
getting their due diligence
in times of doubt;

she resented that death
could not be proud
or punishable by
firing squad;

she listed greed
among her pros,
her bucket list rolled
in a last cigarette;

white hairs matted her face
with a passion death can't steal;
so her eyes swelled pennies
to feel their worth;

a yiskor is said for her
atheist friends,
as a rabbi mouths words
with pedantic sound;

a coffin was sealed
it slips silently
past velvet ropes that guarded
her devalued hopes;

it meanders the ground
like lemmings proceed
instinct as tides
meet tiny feet;

it finally finds a hole,
a place to rest,
a wormy lair that had
spit out the best;

she re-invented
"I'm not going to live forever"

with its icy connotations
that feed the worms;

a tallis knew her coffin's
antiquation; it draped
tziziot on the earth to grow
to tell tales never told.

GOD POLES

they're concentrated;
so much thought went into
delegating them right,
dissipating the
evil energy for
signal towers to talk;

people didn't care,
and there was no reason
to call out anymore;
or act unselfish,
while trying to guide
peaceful sufficient lives;

they're interrogated
by their quiet voices;
and messengers can climb
the towers that go
where neutrons lead to
paths electrons can't find;

they speak frenzied
into phones to be heard;
they negotiate to
beat infinity,
while clicking their heels
to win privacy back;

poles accept signals—
calls idling hands contrive;
they fear people listen
for things to believe in
and purchase calling plans
to talk longer to learn;

if God's ears receive
tiny human clusters;
or pockets of atoms
who try to tap in,
they will listen then as
poles sway free in the wind.

HER NETWORK

it is done well— surreal;
she still watched me in her
approving way;
complex in simplicity,
she pulled at the heart strings
when I saw her;

there my biological
mother did exist, long
after her death;
on Facebook she smiled
and painfully I
could remember;

I shudder to conclude that
her mountain wake worked right;
God must feel good
when things go like he planned so
spirits would get first sight
of refusal;

they'd be seen looking for what
was lost, sad but glad
to have known the missed;
I thought she might be there to
remind me of those things
our time didn't learn;

like when superman visited
his crystals to see
his mother again;
and then I would look between
refractions for tears I cried
for her passing:

once upon a mountain top
14,000 feet up,
where God could see;
I tossed my scoop of ashes
so my mind would sweep free
to remember.

II
RELIGION
{RELATING TO}

HANDS THAT FOLD EMPTY

when impossibilities
yield lives without reason,
God will find an
opportunity;

and turns clocks' hands askew
to filter time;
doves perch precarious
on branches hung for trees;

a force steers bullets' paths
when they strafe to spray;
death's bones are lined
with marrow that says

life's moments are altered
to spin history,
and find heels that
bruise so He might see;

it selects weary saints,
those who surmise
the helpless abused
martyrs He can spare;

hands drag the oceans, they
find fields where death lives;
like trains that stop
can jolt suns to rise;

in doldrums plaintive
angels fear to sing;
a whispered call
steers the albatross
to feed the dying;

it upsets man's plan,
it brings mustard stains;
it plants the seeds in minds
and trains eyes too blind
to see pockets in the sun;

the weakest link barbs
wire that fences shake—
so meek voices matter
when grounds begin to quake

God picks randomly,
and ticks timelessly,
it weaves tapestries
from the silk caskets
worms can never find.

DOVER'S GHOSTS

I would wait
thumbing my hands greedily
for a worthy barrister
at the edge of the cliff;

with his knotty wig
holding me breathlessly,
keeping my confidence
peaked high enough to look;

under rugs, or sneak quick
leaks in chamber pots kept in back
rooms that creak when their
porcelain is pelted softly;

I could wait to coddle foes
and warm irons for them,
to find glows on pasty skins that
knew I'd win my case;

heavy oak doors closed
and my conscience
seized me to sit again
in white-washed pews;

for those he might refuse
to defend 'til my right
to sanctuary ends,
or I die a timely death;

I debate my life with him;
and study the chances
taken when the bar was set
too low for me;

his stitched wig hung
dormant from gravity
greed could buy when
barristers coerced me;

to sit still to pay dues
on all that was owed,
boring me with things
that would be hanged (from the highest cliff)

he'd explain the things I'd never see.

MY EPIPHANY WAS HEARD

I nudged him blithely;
I lifted his Christian doctrines
back up on to the scales where
they'd labored long;
balancing on
self-righteous yard arms that held
me up and measured what was wrong;

I told him plainly
that I believed God was hollow;
a milk- weighing entity
that is churned to
swallow—to crave on rainy days
that come with salient lessons
that teach peaceful ways;

I said God exists
with every person who believes;
I said nothing really persists
but the prayers that fill
the air like cell phone frequencies—
or surreal fingers that reach out to
fix our collars;

I read once that
"God doesn't help those who don't help
themselves"— I thought that people
must meet Him halfway;
he said the bible never says

that, as though the Good Book had bills
God left him to pay;

so I pressed him harder,
I gave him a scenario to weigh;
once I woke up from a coma
(this alone shows that someone prayed)
I'm a string bean now,
a noodle helpless in a chair
with no great prophesies to say;

so in forty years,
after scores of therapy and weights
I sit up straight, remembering my pains
and accomplishments;
but I'm told God was present for
effort I humbly like to claim,
like when thunder claps

and offers latent drops of rain;
they beg one to wonder whether
nature's keeping time;
that reprieve when God has better
insight to nurture the things dead
or relaxed and worn
when people gulp and try to care;

he left knowing I knew my
sense of God better;
I was enlightened by our talk,
God was there if I believed that
I could learn to walk;
he agreed with my acceptance
of his God that knew what I'd say.

GUIDING BANALITY

there was cheesecake and petits fours,
{the tiny cakes I ate on a
French ship when I was four}
and streets were all empty, the cell
phones were mute and hand guns were kiln
to forge strings to lutes;

a man in a homburg asked my
name, he asked if I was on earth
to guide a suicide
or collect on past- due claims;
like repo-men with moribund wings
I'd be sent to garnish;

to seize the things sill in boxes
like Han Solo dolls and Batman
masks that didn't fit well;
faces that quit winning too soon
to know if they lost anyone;
I'd shout it to be heard;

I'd tap loved one's shoulders and hope
they'd feel a chill, I'd tug at their hems
to make them aware
that the game they're playing is fixed;
like spayed dogs or dyslexic gods
who would chant palindromes;

43

I'd turn their losses into wins
and make second-class angel
(like Clarence once played for
George in *it's a wonderful life*);
I'd be Paul Revere's horse pounding
in old north churches calling;

"the reaper's coming! the reaper's coming!"
"the grim reaper's coming at last!"
I'd waddle through with wings
that were forged to their wax, tightly
wound so jacks-in-boxes surprise
you with menacing clowns;

I'd tap harder; I'd shout the words
again, tell them to get out more,
and take dolls and masks from
minty conditions that dusted
in closets so long, to start
fresh like those boxes were torn.

EXPEDITING GREED

you came to Africa
in search of a mission,
and then knelt down, trapped in
position to summon
their god;

she saints in the Congo,
breaching dense parts to tame
docile nether regions
that tangled a brush he'd
tend to;

and leeches swarmed her blood
to ripe submission;
with waves that crest and fall;
he'd tender her well, like
his ships;

worthy conquerors tried
plotting their next moves on
maps salvaged from marshes;
his compass's coordinates
revealed

an alabaster skin;
paled when scales disappeared
from mermaids who would climb
on the rocks to rest as
he'd cheer;

"you came to Africa!"
to be tendered such as
a commission is made,
you can now wait as diamonds
are weighed;

as muddied hip-boots lined
rubbery and sequined scales
sifting hands that wait in
hour -glass shapes to slip in
to wade;

past marshes where cattails
wave lonesome, and arms hang limp
as they seek to drown their
pain; so she dives and breathes
through reeds;

hollowed for his chosen
mission, for the bravest
explorer he could trust
-and commission to work
for free.

DEAD POOLS

I lit a yahrtzeit candle blindly;
I had no premonitions
to what honors dead;
no wicks were cut
or prayers that said;
yet, I knew her spirit danced on the flame;

it wavered, it invented her name;
and heat rose from the glass that held deep
pools of wax that
I feared would drown
in depths wicks would go to see me cry;

throughout the day warm thoughts ensconced me;
then she came, vexing me 'til sundown;
so I prepared
to read a prayer,
precisely at 5:11 I
exhaled 'til smoke lifted from the flame.

NASAL RHYTHMUS

you would claim God was crying
when your thoughts lost their train;
you said that, you couldn't
alleviate the rain;

words you could extoll when you
needed such a conduit
to cognate the pain and suffers
if your world lagged behind;

and then gullies grew
perfections for the drains;
They'd drag steel awnings for
patters to hear in
in your brain;

you'd accuse him of lying
about times your doorbell
rang to alarm you with flaming
sacks dogs' curators left;

you would say He made the
smells that trained ear hairs to
listen intently for drops and
other tapping sounds that came;

when smelly porches
could stand, time could retreat
and teach rain to fall right

and not be bothered
with the pain;

God would accept that if you
made up your mind for Him;
He'd learn the noses that led you
to suffer the smells of rain.

III
POLITICS
{RELATING TO}

SECURITY BACKFIRES (EVERY TIME)

**People have permits to carry
Guns but they don't carry them (the guns)
When they go to the theater;**

if Lincoln had been packing,
he'd have seen his amendment pass;
Kennedy could have seen moon walks
if limousines had gun mounts:

imagine all the permits,
heats packing everywhere;
Lennon could've returned fire
after hollow-point bullets
tore him apart;

presidents could mount
gun cites on their podiums,
tele-prompters would be
ignored and the speech
would become old news:

**This is how it would be,
In self-sufficient democracies—**

it'd ape the old west;
I'd walk in bars with my shooters,
six {or more} ready to parry
back a gunner's fire;

he hasn't read the
latest Time article, doesn't
give a shit about our
"civil liberties;"
doesn't care to see our
phallic pieces or
placate our delusions
of security;

a masked freak is plucked
right out of society's waste bin;
there's nothing to lose, he knows
his shadow will be striped
for our take on eternity;

we'll lift the mask the freakish wear
to conceal and re-peel
gun wrappers who can feel the rights
they have, staring bold
in cites behind hammers;

and then vigilantes'
weapons discharge with harmless cocks;
they're wasted and spent
while the killer comes too fast;

he comes when the sun
gets in your eyes and presence of
mind's weak; he comes
at twilight when work is done,
your SUV idles as you gas up
but where the hell is your gun?
at home, maybe the SUV,
or cumbersomely
placating your crotch?

you heap gas on your credit
card without a care because

you've just worked an honest day
you know paychecks will be there;

a nervous gunman holds you and
the station attendant at gun point;
you smack your forehead
remembering your gun's
at home as your kids play
Russian roulette and you try
to recall if you loaded it:

if I were insecure enough,
if I were so sanctimoniously proud,
if I disavowed taxes
I pay for the TSA,
police, and the rest of the
blessed mercenaries;
I'd get a permit, pay up and finance
another trip for a congressman
to visit the Bahamas;

**I'd be legal and carry it
Near my crotch uncomfortably;**

we'd be inseparable;
all the "bad" guys and dis-
gruntled Americans would carry theirs
illegally, wouldn't give a shit, can't
even comprehend, that I have
gone to great lengths to
protect myself and my family:

**I'd be Yosemite Sam
hunting down varmints
In the Old West;**

I'd be a cartoonish image of a
man with a holster that weighs

him down with 2 loaded barrels,
pathetically thinking he could
defend himself against machine
guns that fire 45 to 60
rpm;

well, I've fired my 1st round;
by the time the 2nd is out of the gun
the drunk sitting next to me
is dead in a pool of his alcohol
infused blood:

His killer has no remorse;
Nothing in heaven or hell can faze him.

he has nothing to live for,
-nothing to die for, and frankly,
I'd like to live to hold my wife again;
more importantly,
I want to live to work again so
I can buy that SUV and trade in
my reins for some keys.

THE PEOPLES' ARMY
(ODE TO THE 2ND AMENDMENT)

and so no one listened, never
heard a word but braved the fight;
still they'd bring their guns to
church, to work, to drink or laugh
at the comedy club.

they'd obliterate all those
armed marauders and kill any infiltrators
to their urban bliss; by
god, they'd fire and reload every
round they had and render their
assailants catatonic;

they'd govern alone and tax
not a dime, and orate their
few lessons so well; they'd have no
police-states to pad their
sell with funny red herring news
print; no cities "finest" to pimp
them out for nothing and then
expect them to cough up rent.

what happens if the laughter ends?
when flying rounds commence and
bullets die to find what angers friends?
it begins with snowballs pelting
the British on king street, that
triangular slab of Boston's

freedom trail, it escalates to
rocks thrown across Gaza's strip;

was Plato wrong— full of babble?
isn't the "punishment which the
wise suffer who refuse to take part
in the government to live under the
government of worse men?"
who are the wise and which men
are worse than them? who does
nothing while evil triumphs to
allow führers to lift their hands.

if Custer's army was great— how
did he get sued if he was the
one who was licensed to kill
any Indian imposing on him?
Sitting Bull wished he had more guns;
regretting that he had but one
life to give for his tribe of
vigilante braves, livid that
he had not rallied stronger
in the early days of May:

reichs and cavalries and
posses did their homework;
they learned the script and
purchased the play to
direct the actor's lines
to claim what's rightfully theirs;
and know what to tell cops
when their guns won't sell
anymore, when the pampered
flag wavers stretch amendments
to even the score;

the army's spoken, its people fed up
with Marie Antoinette's platitudes

and lines that Hitler read on cue;
the government's hands won't reach
that far; so they read Plato and Jefferson
and then invent the rest, a salient clause
grandfather will use to test
the water each time.

A NEW WORLD ORDER
(THE STEPS TO)

<u>The Embryonic age:</u>

they should have gotten it right;
the first time they ate a peach,
and drips fell for virgins
born ostensibly
to preach;

an order was foreseen
so Mayans signed blue-prints,
Jesus drew his curtains back
to see water used to rinse

feet he'd bathe with
rags torn from Ulysses;
the sail that filled wind
like sirens who begged
for pirates to pillage
legs that are pegged
for Egypt's locusts that
left dents to find where
Cain and Abel led;

The Colonial age:

So soon the Masons chiseled;
their cage was gilded, they sought
reasons to keep God in church;

Jefferson swore it led men
astray, like sheep could pen
Christianity; he slid
his quill past happiness,
it kept missing worldly ends;

Franklin laughed at a séance
where kites found currency
a hundred times for what
fathers hoped future
generations could save:

The Newest age (to end all ages)

it hits, age's wrecking ball is
inscribed for us to touch;
with system's in over-haul,
desperately in need of change
for the thrill that felt much
too new; ordered for worlds
custom-made to lose their fit;

the lines are drawn like Spiro-
graphs to link what's left to gain;

they never had it right;
They never had honest fights;
so worlds try to be humane,
treading softly, licking wounds to
feel or compromise what's best;

it becomes a test;
an ageless shot at mercy;
like shell games to never win,
when Ali danced around rings,
swapping salvos with punch-drunk
opponents brought to him; when

he'd let ropes absorb it all,
mocking the dopes that fell
knelt to give "The Greatest"
room to yell and sing about
early days; simple times when
boxers traded knuckles
bare and brash, when hurt was not
for cash and blood could drip
for free from noses too broke
to see what might be learned from fights;

when a citizen band cheered
their buddies on in time and
didn't recant their wines for them.

THE SIXTIES WOLVES

they phased the moon like lemmings
for a piece of history;
when optimism grew
legs and walked away;

they drew from sketching in caves
left for future renderings
of signs protesting the
foe of the hour;

they'd howl like wolves and point
bloodless fangs to save the moon;
they'd find their karma
on the brunt of time;

their nails popped out sharp and scratched
where nature elongated
hairy faces with curled
noses that flare;

moons were still gibbous to man,
werewolves twisted back time's hand
with claws to maul fiendish
smiles man knew;

their skin pimpled with fury
as change rumbled to erupt;
so that earthquakes would learn
the giant's sleeping.

THE GREAT AMERICAN NOVELTY

live with qualms about poetry,
literature and
idolatry;
recall the time you'd spend buying
the copyrights to
apostrophes;

and then he wrote….
and then he spoke….
to shroud your prose in blackened lists
for the blurbs that now
seem too tame to be;

they spied and sent mail to make you
into someone mad
like Uncle Joe
who laughed as you wondered which way
he hunted poets,
so you voted once;

you knew life too well…
it was shown to tell…
but you censored my writing then
in the fifties' days
each dog had one;

they derided your prose with poison
pens that encrypted
America;

then themed the hems to fit the rhymes
and taught you to write
apologies;

so writers could sense....
or dream intense....
as lists were read for what was said
in vagaries;

when you numbered integrity
among caveats
they tried to see;
and books were banned for using "Ns"
when nouns still could squint
at history;

so you would scoff...
and flout their quotes...
scribbling lines copyrighted for
apostrophes.

IRONY'S WOMEN

it all went well; the flappers knew
women's right to bare arms eventually
breeched a state of déjà vu,

when levels of obscenity were achieved
to satiate common men, they
left them wanting more flappy skin;

they could speak with ease,
and swear they'd
shade their eyes and tap their
drinks cockishly waiting for cops
to arrive;

in tubs of gin the flappers lay, they
would wince grins as Carrie
Nation judged whether their
starched-white breasts could
float alone; so

now their descendants gyrate and
hug poles like cobras to fill men;
they show all as sobriety
heeds prohibition and dollars
multiply fruitfully for change the
men won't know.

FINDING DISCIPLINE

if I can't be in a state
of Minnesota nice
every time, assured as
the mosquito bites;

if my wings could melt like
Icarus and hubris was
toned down for my vain, petty
pursuits of happiness;

my messianic mantra
could hold my tongue from
writhing free, babbling loose
to count cribbage points piously;

my Norse heritage gives me
confidence, a sense that
I could do better, find softer
feet to wash than Jesus did;

but I draw a line close to
my exfoliated, scaly skin;
I'll read Prospero's books
written for the tempestuous

looks I've felt; back when Atlas
shouldered the world, with his thumbs
in fists for salvation's brand;
they feel out to need me much,

more than merchants ever did;
I kneel, staggered by richer men;
I hang shylock's scales to weigh
Losses in discipline.

FIFTEEN MINUTES OF EASEMENT

6:26: I hear the plow
scraping my street
with a dulled sound;
it sprinkles pavement
with salt and sand
to give cars a winter coat;

city's drones my taxes don't name—
will clear my streets
but shake my sleep;
and the cold
dry air tries to quiet
as they hang their breath
out to dry for me;

relentlessly they're
emboldened by their
boots, their coats
and lime-green vests;
winter's toy soldiers
might need a crank
to warm one day when…

They're still out there;
glints of sun follow,
it dances on those vests
to highlight paths they graded;

6:41 sounds more pleasing
chiseling the cars' window frames;
insolent owners offer the
workers a last chance at fame;

the lime light shade's past me
and swaths of sun seal
my eyes staring out
from curtain's with pleats that
fold when snow drifts too far.

FRAYED ROPES

who counts when fibers fray;
when flags stay in the middle
of lanyards, poles feel breezes
touch each day;

salutes tell its story,
shading eyes that lost their way;
how often will the top show
emptiness;

I mourn a flag suppressed
and America chides its
tolerance but honors
who's killed less,
freedom's advocates;

how many times will headlines
cause me to clench my fists
in an anger that I thought I could
control? like delusions of pursuing
happiness warm guns missed;
scraps of words spun viciously
like the gun whose chamber's bare;
holding eyes open to shoot straight,
personalizing their stories told

so flags could feel their draft;

when the staffs are empty and
apathy has claimed its soul;
loose lanyards clip the wind
as handguns are banned in places
where signs are not as old;

as clauses for militia grow
freer than states they guard;
on edges frayed for lanyard's
follow through; its pulleys know
to stop at points I'll always see.

BELT LOOPS

I grind my teeth; soon I closed my eyes
To pay my bills;
I'd hesitate like a frog's tongue
before a fly;

I learn slowly things money buys,
frivolous slips
by weakened wills;

I should deride myself to be
me someday soon;
I'll agree to coupon buys
that deflate things;

my squalor's bonds are tightly wound,
they rap lightly
when my shoulders shrug to send me
on light spending sprees.

CANINE FIGURES

I walked so briskly the slower paths
people stroll down,
and then age wears time wrong for laughs;
it sews the gaps generations
have tendered for centuries
to help canines pass;

and people stay seven steps behind
those dogs trained to walk their age,
with their deeds that nourish the earth;
they grow like children and dot the eyes
that masters tease from birth
of rabid mongrels who can roam the parks

for righteous masters jogging on
narrow European heels,
turning in their steps as they chase
after dogs chomping their bits of pain;
I watch collars choke them hard
so they'll learn to answer by name;

I can see them come from walks of life
populating many for the
few patrons of tethered leashes;
to learn things their dogs already knew;
the generations gap deeply through
park paths finding ways to my
window sill so I might hear;

dogs could pant after, lapping swill
that sweats off Europe's sharp heels;
and leashes soften pelts of rain;
when clouds' impasses diminish days,
dogs run free on narrow paths
to alleys they should fear.

IV
FRIENDSHIP
{RELATING TO}

THE FLOATING BRIDGE

your vibes did resonate
with me,
like smudged windows look out
to see;
if moons could drip mist for
starless
skies and wander silent
asking
why paints create views to
see sight;

you'd predict what was the
best course
my canvas could take;
you'd help
me make a perfect world
for you,
my tender cousin who'd
find her
fate if I should find words
too late;

and plow the fields that find
small birds
that mock and sing off key,
with brush
tails weighted for smaller
beaks that
peck to nudge you awake;

where tails
of cats would sway to tease
the winds;

breezing past marshy shakes
I see,
the reeds that hide those tails
from me;
they blow the cattail's seeds
toward wind
for my relation to sketch
the night's
moons lovers could show.

LIMESTONE RUINS

the young ace mixologist
was a friend of mine;
"Commander" spiked my drinks with tea,
he went to school for
a brief slice of time during
which I would drink my
weight in ale dispensed across
a bridge he'd built me;

I passed viaducts there, the
untamed thoroughfare;
alone I could amble in
my temporary
saloon of legends urbane;
myths that had grown
that Commander cut lemons
back there in wedged shapes;

we'd sling guns from hips and shoot
those who drank on sight;
spurs would spin—they'd jingle my walk
to swagger in
and push swinging doors to meet
their hinges' greed;
fanning stale popcorn smells that
beer vied to exceed;

we franchised dreams; I'd look
in on Commander

for the lessons he learned for me;
I'd see the classroom
antics with serious
disciples of
ace mixology learning
to bounce drunks on sight;

he'd be tilting back plastic
seminar chairs
that would mold a tavern for bar
keeps of brand new
dispensaries
who learned their trade;
one day he would offer mugs
of kindness to me.

MANIC CONCESSIONS

he came close to living
along banks
of the Mississippi;
he'd have lived
in his van without roaches
eating bread;

his meals were
of cold government cheese;
it's yellow
corners splintering through
trees, his dull
butter knife would smear jam:

and then a
November chill tousled
his neck's scruff;
with chattered teeth he'd ask
how much to
room until his cheese thawed;

he'd invent
elusive antidotes
for roaches;
we'd spread jam in the sink
with that dull
knife; he offered to ease

their pain with
ways they might outwit games
he'd create;
we'd leave it dark,
and go to the
spaces his band would play;

we'd return
and throw on kitchen lights;
the roaches
would scatter like feces;
we'd focus
cans and charge in to spray;

he'd tally
them up like Vietnam's
reported dead;
and number in a stink bug
like cattle
were on slow days it's said;

my sofa
was stuffed with roaches
probably;
so we'd sit and relish
our kills that
stained the sink with rings;

we relaxed
after our nightly raid;
we ate
voraciously
Swiss cake rolls from a pail
of snow like
two Kafkaesque kings.

FOOT NOTES

they knew the right chords;
instinctively the musicians
jangled and blew;
acoustic guitars played
as two, in time so a flautist knew
for what it's worth;

their fingers would dance
respectively, they'd impress frets
for foot joints too;
a flute's quivering
wrists had ended; their holder gasps
breathless in thanks,

the acoustics would
let him know it's the end; then a
soft- spoken man
starts up like Tom Waits,

he's on cue to chant blues with "no
expectations;"
for stones that roll to
gather the breath to flute again
or diminish chords
with a tambourine;
she offered then to keep time for
the tenormen.

MICHAEL P AMRAM

SEARCHING FOR BLADES

their voices were just their patter,
idle gossip didn't mean a thing;
words aspired to force friends
to cough dimes to spare;

they never felt tongues wrap glib
words in parcels never meant to send;
only the best time heals
what learns to pass for friends;

still great minds convene secretly
in booths; words won't fathom their beers,
they skim heads and gulp to
toast so adjournment nears;

they hunch and dine furtively,
for conversations kept off record;
like a tape would hear the
thoughts they scratched to see;

impartial waitresses brought food
and catch tips as their tray is cleared;
they look down evasively
as men hope their heads will clear;

when politics or religion
is too thick for their pitcher's spout;
when sex serves innuendos
for conversations course;

then final reparations see
collusions cast so friends won't divorce;
hatchets bury in their plots
marking booths as a recourse.

END ZONES (FOR AARON)

he went long;
he hid me well
as he ran to his end;

gridded fields chalked the
bending winded blades;
white grass would prod
to lodge in cleated shoes;

he danced intensely
towards goals with zones;
he carried the ball
long and ran to lose;

he wrestled
until he fell,
wearing thin the seeds sown;

he never spoke of me—
always kept blind;
his legs ran to
pace super bowl fame;

he protected his wife
and family;
my siblings
who shared half with me;

he fumbled;
fate went long to
receive him with a grace;

defensive ends will 'punch'
offensive lines;
tickling grass
with three-point dance steps;

he hid me like a ball
is kept under
wings worn wrong like
a mask shields a face.

HOSTING PERFECTION

you polished tables
and sent out your shoes;
to the local kids for dimes
and a buff, like new
pairs you bought at the
thrift stores they patronize;

your shoes shuffled a
pace that favored feats
of ghosts of friends who'd haunt
your floors; they're clean with
ripe Lemmon scent the
planks would creak for you;

a bed's lain thick with
the coats of your guests;
when your party lulled
you spoke, you slurred words
and resigned as a source of
transportation home;

your reasons abated
the breath that could cloud your
shoes' toothy smiles;
liqueurs found caches
for the crème de menthe bottles
bathing tables in
green;

walls surrounded
you with their glass menagerie;
still your toasts were made
laughing, needling you
to be anything but
rude; so you gripped your
chair as guests thanked you;

for the good times their shoes had
with imbedded coats
and toothless smiles;
for tables reflecting its host,
and soon, when village kids
are in bed you sigh.

V
MARRIAGE
{RELATING TO}

THE FEAR OF MATTRESS NAGS

I could fit our mattress cover
unassisted;
I no longer needed my wife,
her loving touch
and shrewd guidance were no longer
required to
pull our bed cushion's edges tight;

it'd slide on the mattress with the
tricks that I'd learned
from her head games and the dirty
deeds she'd done;
she made them clean so I'd allow
her flowery
pillow cases and duvet slips;

her orange and red lacey satin
sheets I'd apply
to sleep and try more masculine
ones instead;
just to hear her voice moan at night
and smother her
coolly so nothing's said;

she gasps to give
her crimson mattress stains whiffs of
cigarette breath;
she rasps her name in monotones
repeatedly;

intently lulling me to sleep
with puffs of smoke;

rings rise from her shrunken mouth like
eyelets on shoes,
with their shiny round grommet holes
hung for mattress
tags the lock jawed sleepwalker fears;
her eyes settle,
they cut like knives...balanced...shifting...

darting askew;
as her duvet dusts her bunnies

out in the light
so orange sheets amuse crimson
in gentle nights;
her hand goes limp like a puppet
who's mastered one

of the thin strings that soft mattress
covers will grow;
she stares into death and pretends
to close her eyes—
while her lips gurgle the final
nags I must know;
I pull our cover tight... again.

SUSTENANCE

she kept a jar of fish
on the cupboard;
it tempted me with its
blue gefillte
logo that would dance
horas in the
bright kitchen space;

its orange queues
of fish had carrots
anointing them;
regal like Jesus
who once was king;
they mimicked hymns that
her hums could sing;

then conglomerate
to make her see;
they'd puzzle fuses
so lights could bounce
from white floors to be
my amalgams;

they'd distort inside
the jar to me;
they'd show how low bars
will go to set
a hoarder's cravings free;
through tempered glass

stashed away from sun;

light at windows
whose blinds are drawn closed;
slats right to left
in case Israel peeks in
to see the jar
that collected dust;

fingers would point
and dust our blinds
to release her
from mistrust that spared
those fish, a fear that
kept them there for spite;
in cupboard nooks
where hoarders would shine.

BALANCING TRUST

I would slice our sponge
with a knife;
she'd say
I might want to wait
for her to
wipe it;

edgy and clean, "too
sharp" my wife
would say;
she didn't trust me
if tasks were
simple;

like a kitchen's vows
should transcend
marriages;
so knives were allowed
to rust in
the drain;

Where apathy thinks
And lettuce
Leaves feign
the floaters that wink
for couples
to fight;

so I sliced our sponge,
vindictive
for meat;
and hoped the dullest
blades concede
defeat.

HER LESSONS IN PENURIOUSNESS

I once said if I drifted on a raft
one day I would want her there;
I said anyone should feel lucky to
have her on board, staring out
meekly, in prisms from her rubber corners
reflecting Pacific sun;

she had an obsession; she'd ration
all food so scrupulously;
she would plant her irrational seeds
to coffer proclivity;
she'd keep a ledger of the smacks that
passed by her conscripted lips;

I once rehashed The Great Depression;
I said people waited in lines,
she would not have to sieve through their sorrow;
she'd always eaten 3 meals
doled out rigidly in squares for her;
I'd shake off her poverty

and realized it still clings like pieces of
dried meat on bones that were gnawed;
her plate was always spotless,
her utensils in perfect alignment;
but she'd harp on me to do
the same to have food for the next night;

she'd always nag me to use
the daylight, like we were in London
when the Blitzkrieg was raining;
one night she used a flashlight to read a
book at twilight; she could squint
her eyes to lower monthly light bill;

it had become a challenge
to save cereal or electricity,
a trial to prove how long
the box or bulb could remain alive;
I long observed her lessons of thrift
and concluded her frugalness had to be.

VI
AGEING
{RELATING TO}

THE PINCH SLIPPERS

she gives me an extra
pair to wear
around when I can't bend;
I am ready, in case
my toes curl
and my feet slip to the end;

when the spare shoes would hide
under beds;
or desks to hamper my
dress; so I
won't shuffle my days with
dusty feet;

when the neglect comes
so abrupt,
peeling off zippers dust
covers made—
and gauged fits of spares she
wagered to trust;

so slippery slopes would
yield for me,
like toes that hanged the feet
that would cross
to know all the house shoes
dying lost:

drape's now flutter the
curtains drawn;
wind teases them like the
retrievals
from the beds and desk that
kept me lost.

LABORS OF FRUIT

she intended to live
to a ripe age;
like a banana does
with spots and sweet
smells that would arouse what
senses were dulled;

she wanted to host at
a party when
hers were ripe, for her friends
with chattering
teeth and brown liver spots;
their donkey tails
could pin themselves low, hung

from limbo poles
over deep pits of flames;
shriveled ankles
wade to shimmy and flute
skirts for the coals
that burn hot for the game;

so they would move
the party to a grassy knoll
so asses came;
and then held their sagging
still as they breathed
last rites to die.

HIBERNATION

it's 2 AM, I see trees sway;
they touch me in my bed
and scratchy leaves plot the moonlight
that filters dreams through my head;

then streets slick with shadowed sweat
leave wrinkles in my sheets;
like rainstorms tramped heavy to cage
blissful nights from whence I'd dream;

still 3AM finds dogs who bark
and streetlights to listen hard;
I lay in misted nights of sleep
with perspiration's darkness;

to teach the rain rhythms to
fall; where winds howl and
dogs were trained to sleep
so sheets wrap me lightly;

4AM winks weak, but enough
for me to feel its gain;
I'm lost to sleep for the hours by
while nature feeds me its
dampened cues as wasted eyes blink
at clocks digital lights;
bending beams I will prism to
compromise where I sleep.

IRRITANTS

I don't have a rolling clock that's
white, with black numbered time;
I never saw a pocket watch
with lint trapped in folds of seams;

its blinks turning wheels to learn,
notes that you scribbled for things to do;
fits of nerves that click too numb
and work to tease my mind to play;

when the beds began to listen
to the birds that can catch worms;
heads begin to chafe its pillows,
rolling its eyes to start the day.

A JUMP IN LIFE

a sigh admits rest and asks
'w*hys*' for my younger days;
the way pain felt when
it brushed like flies;
it's half a century in now
and life has slowed enough
to sneak listens to
the farts brains hum;

low testosterone might be,
when the gym's a chore and
fitness drops low in
priority;
my feet *pop* to tease with me
they feel swell in the rain;
they're boney and red
so my shoes fit;

I won't be playing 'pull my
finger' when I get old;
children would hear joints
slide fluid less;
they won't be amused by sounds
of a mime passing gas
with white face paint thick and
twisting to laugh;

sciatica pimps for me,
it hunches of the pains
to know that I limp;

So I gait past
life changes and pee freely,
I 'man down' and straddle
my cane to walk by
my former selves:

you 'retire' chasing health, days
time no longer affords;
if regrets can strain out
finer rewards.

A SCHOOL OF GERONTOLOGY

they fit you well,
the turquoise bracelets that
hung limply as
you danced horas alone;

you clapped your hands
and then your anklets jangled;
like the keys cuffed
on your wrist made you known;

your guests learned to peel
the sagging holds of skin
under your arms when
I'd lecture you;

about the books
on scientology
for the birthday wish
that was long belated;

you'd clap one hand
and kick the other shoe
up so your skirt
would trust the floor intuitively;

you'd remember guests
bragging about their dreams
remembered
on anniversaries.

VII
TECHNOLOGY
{RELATING TO}

BOLDER REALITIES

I want to know what's real to
touch, tempting what I see
swirl random to
feel what's integral to be;
so virtually all is
virtual to see;

please say if it's righteous
and virtuous to know;
give me rocks to polish
so I can watch them grow;

the 70s stones could wait
so real to the touch
in a box with their
unconditional love that
was always virtual
and self-deluded;

and the pet had novelty
with its booklet and slick
gray stone fingers
could imprint smooth, softer than
those loyal pets who sat
through history.

MICHAEL P AMRAM

AS WHEELS TURNED

when words came streaming past—
2050 blazed boldly
across a sky;
bright minds would save time to
fill their hard drives' with thoughts
to become recycle
bins that left space
to write encrypted things;

for scholars who would lie
down for time's defamation
of things they knew
once, when life could kindle
thought processes to learn
and maybe glow; they'd burn
out in front of
computer screens that flicked

at neon-green cursors
blinking away as the soft
chips rifted to slip
silently away
to the larger wheels of
more distant gains, when gray
mattered and earth was ripe
to plant seeds that
grew once to stem a brain;
chips would infuse hackers' eyes;
they would blink twice

for "no," their hands reached out
for mice that could click once
for "yes," they'd never wait
for glances that
reasoned eyes with logic
or human rationale;

they'd just pry at an
ability to think; it
atrophied, molted
and fell away, like tales
of Orwellian rats;
tethered to a box when
wheels spun new; thoughts
were few so
rodents think
today.

EVOLUTION LOST ANOTHER TALE

does anyone remember when
words could sense cars' pistons pause?
they'd wait in texts to send,
and what became of the safe
memory banks, the graphite
pens that held unrequited thoughts;

there were no distractions then
there were no distractions when,
fuzzy dice hung warm in
mirrors amusing as they knew
your face; they heard words you said
and the world could slow to race;

do you ever re-think the
calls you made; you'd pound steering
wheels for the roads you raged;
when bumpers were tapped abrupt
so your middle finger rose
and anger was conveyed?

there were no distractions then
there were no distractions when,
channels broke for truckers
and good buddies were apprised
of what was ahead of them
with humored passivity;

does anyone reflect on when
twisted fenders were things to
avoid and cell phone didn't
justify the means to your end;
and the world revolved fine
at times without you.

THE KEY WORDS (WERE IN TEXT)

they twisted the key at the party
that stopped their brains
from running;

it was February, 1980;
computers were
taking charge;

brains checked out while studio
54 had a
last hurrah;

a sizzling sound was heard,
and dancers bowed
to recall;

the golden age when minds shifted
autonomous
to their train;

they bid farewell to logic,
machines would rent
space to play;

with memories of thinking times,
back when disco
danced on time;

before "i's" on every pad
would watch bigger
brothers climb;

and fingers snapped for the beat
to be limber
to type text;

"can anyone find what's missing"
like the chip that
turned the key;

so their computers could tell them
to re-invent
yesterdays.

IF THE BRAIN CLICKS (FORGET IT)

I aspire to be a robot
the firewall insisted; it
instructed a last chance to
blink and recede from my machine;
subliminally pitching some
fonts to intimidate me for
the next secured wall I should
navigate past; it had nails that tapped

human thought, an archaic concept
that couldn't even compete with them;
the brains went away when 8-track
tapes were pulled from the bins to be
replaced with the shiny discs that
wouldn't click to the next track;

digitally burned, they're infinitely
faultless with subliminal sounds
designed to close ears and render
them incapable to hear or use
prompts they'd already learned;

"so prove you're human" computers
brazenly ask in dimmed, eschewed
alpha-numeric codes you change
if they're phrased too cryptically;
you may even listen as it's
read by a voice programmed and trained

to weaken the days; when people
still answered their phones and trusted
their minds, when they'd still realize
machines are not infallible
and can't replicate human sense;

so they stand mute, helpless and dumbed
by computer's fascist grip,
they wait for an estranged 8-track
to offer its click.

SYSTEM DOLDRUMS

her voice was austere and
I sensed encrypted codes;
vacant, tracing vibrations
to find where I sat;

she asked if I was
who I thought I was and
told me to affirm this by
pressing a one;

I chose a day and
a time to come live for
an interview at a place
that exists somewhere:

I'll go to my date;
I imagine a robot
will shake my hand and then scratch
its head with pinched hands;

I'll show up early
to imprint something to
pull my name ahead in their
race to fill a job;

or a slot where a
computer glitch has paused
for technology to lag
ahead at the tape:

so a job was lost,
automated for the
convenience, wire tapped
for efficiency;

to throw the race blind
while maintaining a pace,
its voices recorded to
test dexterity;

modulating voices
to learn tenacity
levels you have to follow
non-human cues;

send in the clones now—
the computers filling
their shoes to forge a lead
for prosperity.

THE POETRY JAR

paper notes cling together with
lessons ready to unfold;
an empty fish jar holds snippets
of notations urging me
to my words;

they're what prescience could spite,
wisdom the jar might reveal;
its threads through crusted paths
to know its seal:

ingeniously designed, fraught
with words subliminal;
but my hands are torn together
tracing my palms;

hiding verses, making
procrastination tell;
they're submitted like paths to treasure—
maps I followed would lead me
past where lines break to seem real.